CHILDREN'S COOKERY
NATURALLY

BY

VIRG AND JO LEMLEY

WILDERNESS HOUSE
11129 Caves Highway
Cave Junction, OR 97523

© copyright 1980 by WILDERNESS HOUSE
ALL RIGHTS RESERVED

ISBN 0-931798-05-1

WILDERNESS HOUSE BOOKS

- **CHILDREN'S COOKERY — NATURALLY**
  NOW CHILDREN HAVE FUN LEARNING TO COOK WITH FOODS THAT ARE BEST FOR THEM.

- **SOYBEAN COOKERY**
  BEAT TODAY'S RISING FOOD COSTS. LEARN TO COOK DELIGHTFULLY APPETIZING, ALL-AMERICAN DISHES FOR PENNIES.

- **ZUCCHINI COOKERY**
  BURIED IN ZUCCHINI? THIS IS THE BOOK FOR YOU.

FROM WILDERNESS HOUSE___

WE BRING TO YOU THE JOY OF COOKING DELIGHTFULLY APPETIZING DISHES AS ONLY WHOLE NATURAL FOODS CAN MAKE THEM. WE ARE SHARING WITH YOU AN ADVENTURE IN LEARNING TO COOK WITH THOSE THINGS THAT ARE CLOSEST TO NATURE. FROM YOUR EFFORTS MAY YOU AND YOUR FAMILY BE HEALTHIER AND HAPPIER.

TABLE OF CONTENTS

WHAT ARE NATURAL FOODS? ___ 1

WHY NATURAL FOODS? ___ 1

BE A WISE COOK ___ 2

BE A GOOD COOK ___ 2

BE A SAFE COOK ___ 3

SOME NATURAL FOODS YOU MAY BE USING ___ 4

SALADS

SUMMER DELIGHT ___ 7
GARDEN SALAD ___ 8
OLD KING COLE SLAW ___ 9
HAWAIIAN SALAD ___ 10
FRUIT BASKET ___ 11
POLLY'S POTATO SALAD ___ 12
STRAWBERRY SPECIAL ___ 14

MAIN DISHES

BROWN RICE ___ 15
STIR FRY ORIENTAL ___ 16
MISH MASH ___ 17
POCKET BREAD ___ 18
POCKET BREAD FILLINGS ___ 20
QUESADILLA ___ 21
OMELET ___ 22
OMELET FILLINGS ___ 23
PIZZA SAUCE ___ 24
SUNSHINE PIZZA ___ 25
RAINBOW MACARONI ___ 26

DESSERTS

MERINGUE FLUFF	27
RICE PUDDING	28
GRANDMA'S APPLESAUCE	29
STRAWBERRY FLUFF	30
CRUNCHY GRANOLA BARS	31
LEMON CUSTARD ICE CREAM	32
CAROB SWIRL ICE CREAM	33
ANGEL PUFFS	34

SNACKS

TRAIL MIX	35
POPCORN	36
POPCORN BALLS	37
GRANOLA	38
CRUNCHY PEANUT BUTTER	39
SNAPPY CHEESE CRACKERS	40
CINNAMON NUT BUNS	42
PARTY SURPRISE	43
FRUIT LEATHER	44

MAGIC MIX

MAGIC MIX	46
BANANA NUT BREAD	47
PANCAKES	48
APPLESAUCE HONEY SYRUP	49
HONEY BUTTER	49
PEANUT BUTTER COOKIES	50
APPLE MUFFINS	51
CREPES	52
CREPE FILLINGS	53
CORNBREAD	54

BE AN ACCURATE COOK	55
SOME COOKING TERMS	56

WHAT ARE NATURAL FOODS?

Natural foods are simply the closest thing to nature.

A carrot from your garden is more natural than one you buy at the store. The carrot from the store is more natural than one that is in the can.

Raw wheat is a grain. It is more natural than whole wheat flour that has been ground. Whole wheat flour is more natural than bleached white flour.

Orange juice you juice yourself, is more natural than fresh orange juice from the store. Fresh orange juice is more natural than frozen orange juice.

WHY NATURAL FOODS?

Food is the fuel to make your body go as well as the building blocks to help your body grow.

Natural foods are higher in vitamins and minerals than other foods. They also have natural enzymes which helps your body to use all of the food you eat.

Your body was made to use food in its natural state. Processing, coloring, and adding preservatives is man's, not nature's, idea of food.

Eating foods that work with your body will help keep you healthy and happy.

BE A WISE COOK

READ THE LABELS WELL WHEN SELECTING FOODS.

SELECT FOODS WITHOUT ANY ARTIFICIAL COLORING.

SELECT FOODS WITHOUT ANY ARTIFICIAL FLAVORING.

SELECT FOODS WITHOUT ANY PRESERVATIVES.

SELECT FOODS CLOSEST TO NATURE.

BE A GOOD COOK

WASH YOUR HANDS BEFORE YOU START TO COOK.

READ YOUR RECIPE THROUGH TO THE END.

LAY OUT ALL OF THE FOODS YOU WILL NEED.

LAY OUT ALL OF THE EQUIPMENT YOU WILL NEED.

FOLLOW THE DIRECTIONS FOR EACH RECIPE.

MEASURE INGREDIENTS EXACTLY.

CLEAN UP AS YOU GO.

WASH AND DRY ALL OF THE UTENSILS YOU HAVE USED.

LEAVE YOUR KITCHEN NEAT AND TIDY.

BE A SAFE COOK

LIFT THE LIDS OF HOT PANS AWAY FROM YOU.

TURN THE HANDLES OF PANS TOWARDS THE BACK OF THE STOVE.

USE A WOODEN SPOON WHEN STIRRING FOODS THAT ARE HOT.

USE A CUTTING BOARD WITH YOUR KNIFE.

USE POT HOLDERS WHEN HANDLING HOT PANS.

HAVE DRY HANDS WHEN YOU PLUG IN AN APPLIANCE.

ALWAYS HAVE THE LID ON THE BLENDER BEFORE YOU TURN IT ON.

SOME NATURAL FOODS YOU MAY BE USING

RAW NUTS — A NUTRITIOUS FOOD THAT ADDS FLAVOR AND TEXTURE TO YOUR DISHES.

BROWN RICE — A WHOLE GRAIN FILLED WITH NUTRITION. WHITE RICE HAS BEEN STRIPPED OF BRAN AND MUCH OF ITS FOOD VALUE.

WHOLE WHEAT FLOUR — GROUND WHEAT IN ITS NATURAL FORM, LOADED WITH GOOD THINGS FOR YOUR BODY.

YOGURT — A GOOD FOOD WITH LOTS OF NATURAL ENZYMES TO HELP YOUR BODY USE ITS FOOD.

CHEESE — NATURAL CHEESE IS MADE WITH RAW MILK WITHOUT ANY ARTIFICIAL COLORING OR PRESERVATIVES. MAKING CHEESE IS AN ART AS OLD AS NATURE ITSELF.

HONEY — NATURE'S SWEETENER. SO GOOD FOR YOU — AND — A REAL ENERGY FOOD.

UNREFINED SAFFLOWER OIL — PRESSED WITHOUT THE USE OF CHEMICALS OR SOLVENTS.

CAROB POWDER — SIMPLY THE GROUND POD OF THE CAROB TREE. HIGH IN NUTRITION AND EASY FOR YOUR BODY TO USE.

SEA SALT   EVAPORATED BY THE
                SUN TO BE EASIER FOR
                YOUR BODY TO USE.

BAKING   THERE IS A BAKING
POWDER   POWDER AVAILABLE
                AT YOUR LOCAL
                HEALTH FOOD STORE
                THAT DOES NOT HAVE
                HARMFUL CHEMICALS
                IN IT.

SALADS

SUMMER DELIGHT

① | 1 CUP BLACKBERRIES
1 CUP STRAWBERRIES
1 CUP BANANAS — CUT IN SLICES | COMBINE IN A BOWL.

② | $\frac{1}{2}$ CUP PLAIN YOGURT
2 TABLESPOONS HONEY | STIR HONEY INTO YOGURT.

③ COMBINE FRUIT AND DRESSING.

SERVES: 4

GARDEN SALAD

1.
   - 1/2 CUP LEMON JUICE
   - 1/2 CUP WATER
   - 1/2 CUP HONEY
   - 1/8 TEASPOON SEA SALT

   PUT IN A SAUCEPAN. HEAT UNTIL IT STARTS TO BUBBLE.

2. 1 PACKAGE UNFLAVORED GELATIN

   PUT IN A BOWL. STIR HOT LIQUID INTO GELETIN. STIR UNTIL THE GELATIN IS DISSOLVED.

3. PUT MIXTURE INTO THE REFRIGERATOR UNTIL THE GELATIN BEGINS TO GET FIRM.

4. 1/2 CUP CELERY — CHOP INTO FINE PIECES.

5. 1/2 CUP CARROT — CHOP INTO FINE PIECES.

6. 1/2 CUP CABBAGE — CHOP INTO FINE PIECES.

7. STIR CHOPPED VEGETABLES INTO GELATIN THAT IS ALMOST FIRM.

8. REFRIGERATE UNTIL FIRM.

SERVES: 4

OLD KING COLE SLAW

1. 1 EGG — PUT IN BLENDER. PLACE LID ON. TURN TO MEDIUM. COUNT TO 30.

2. 1 TABLESPOON VINEGAR — POUR THROUGH HOLE IN THE TOP OF THE LID. COUNT TO 15 WHILE STILL BLENDING.

3. $\frac{1}{2}$ CUP SAFFLOWER OIL — KEEP BLENDING. DRIZZLE IN AS YOU COUNT TO 30.

4. 1 TABLESPOON HONEY / PINCH OF SEA SALT — ADD WHILE STILL BLENDING.

5. PUT IN REFRIGERATOR TO CHILL.

6. 4 CUPS CABBAGE — SLICE VERY THIN. PUT IN A LARGE SALAD BOWL.

7. $1\frac{1}{2}$ CUPS DICED APPLES / $\frac{1}{2}$ CUP RAISINS / $\frac{1}{2}$ CUP PEANUTS — MIX TOGETHER WITH THE CABBAGE.

8. TOSS WITH CHILLED DRESSING.

SERVES: 6

HAWAIIAN SALAD

① | 1 CUP ORANGE JUICE
    1/2 CUP HONEY | PUT IN A SAUCEPAN. HEAT UNTIL IT STARTS TO BUBBLE.

② | 1 PACKAGE UNFLAVORED GELATIN | PUT IN A BOWL. STIR HOT LIQUID INTO GELATIN. STIR UNTIL GELATIN IS DISSOLVED.

③ PUT MIXTURE INTO REFRIGERATOR UNTIL THE GELATIN BEGINS TO GET FIRM.

④ | 1 CUP DICED ORANGE
    1/4 CUP PLAIN YOGURT
    1/4 CUP COCONUT FLAKES | STIR INTO GELATIN THAT IS ALMOST FIRM.

⑤ REFRIGERATE UNTIL FIRM.

SERVES: 4

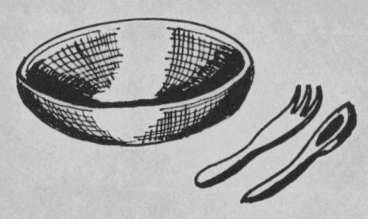

FRUIT BASKET

1. | 2 SMALL CANTALOPE | — CUT IN HALF. CLEAN SEEDS OUT.

2. | 1 PEAR | — CUT IN HALF. CLEAN OUT CORE. CUT INTO CUBES.

3. | 1 BANANA | — SLICE THIN.

4. | 1 ORANGE | — PEEL. PULL SLICES APART. CUT EACH SLICE INTO 3 PARTS.

5. | 1 CUP SEEDLESS GRAPES |

6. MIX THE PEAR, BANANA, AND ORANGE TOGETHER IN A LARGE BOWL. STIR IN GRAPES.

7. FILL EACH CANTALOPE HALF WITH $\frac{1}{4}$ OF THE MIXTURE.

8. | $\frac{1}{2}$ CUP PLAIN YOGURT / $\frac{1}{4}$ CUP HONEY | — MIX TOGETHER.

9. PUT 3 TABLESPOONS OF DRESSING OVER EACH FRUIT BASKET.

10. TOP WITH A PRETTY MINT LEAF FROM YOUR GARDEN.

SERVES: 4

POLLY'S POTATO SALAD

① | 6 MEDIUM POTATOES
    2 QUARTS WATER
    1 TEASPOON SEA SALT

PUT IN A COVERED PAN. TURN HEAT TO HIGH UNTIL POTATOES START TO BOIL. TURN HEAT DOWN. COOK FOR 25 MINUTES.

② | 6 EGGS
    1 QUART WATER

PUT IN A COVERED PAN. TURN HEAT TO HIGH UNTIL EGGS START TO BOIL. <u>TURN HEAT OFF.</u> LET SIT FOR 20 MINUTES.

③ | 2 EGGS

BEAT EGGS WHILE YOU COUNT TO 60.

④ | $\frac{1}{4}$ CUP VINEGAR
    1 TEASPOON SEA SALT
    $\frac{1}{2}$ TEASPOON PEPPER

ADD VINEGAR, SALT, AND PEPPER. BEAT AGAIN WHILE YOU COUNT TO 60.

⑤ | 1 CUP SAFFLOWER OIL

WHILE STILL BEATING, <u>SLOWLY</u> POUR IN SAFFLOWER OIL.

(A BLENDER MAY BE USED IN PLACE OF THE BEATERS FOR STEPS ③, ④, AND ⑤).

POLLY'S POTATO SALAD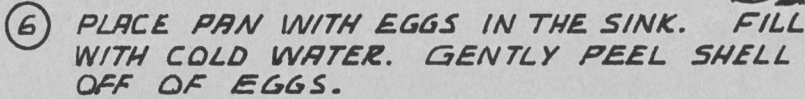

⑥ PLACE PAN WITH EGGS IN THE SINK. FILL WITH COLD WATER. GENTLY PEEL SHELL OFF OF EGGS.

⑦ CHOP EGGS. PUT IN BOTTOM OF LARGE BOWL.

⑧ | $\frac{1}{2}$ CUP CHOPPED GREEN ONIONS | ADD TO EGGS.

⑨ CUT TWO WARM POTATOES INTO CUBES. PLACE IN BOWL WITH EGGS AND ONIONS.

⑩ SPLASH $\frac{1}{2}$ CUP OF THE DRESSING OVER THE POTATOES.

⑪ REPEAT STEP ⑩ UNTIL YOU HAVE USED ALL OF YOUR POTATOES AND DRESSING.

⑫ MIX WELL. SERVE WARM OR CHILL IN THE REFRIGERATOR TO SERVE COLD.

SERVES: 6

STRAWBERRY SPECIAL

① | 3 CUPS STRAWBERRIES | RINSE. TAKE OFF STEMS.

② | $\frac{1}{4}$ CUP HONEY
   | $\frac{1}{2}$ CUP COTTAGE CHEESE | PUT IN BLENDER. TURN ON HIGH. BLEND UNTIL SMOOTH. OR YOU MAY USE AN ELECTRIC BEATER.

③ PUT BERRIES IN BOWL. POUR SAUCE OVER BERRIES.

SERVES: 4

MAIN DISHES

BROWN RICE

① 2 3/4 CUPS WATER
  1 TEASPOON SEA SALT
  1 TABLESPOON
       SAFFLOWER OIL

BRING TO A BOIL IN A SAUCEPAN.

② 1 CUP BROWN RICE

ADD TO BOILING WATER.

③ TURN HEAT TO <u>LOW</u>. COVER PAN WITH LID. COOK FOR 45 MINUTES. DON'T PEEK.

MAKES: 3 CUPS

STIR FRY ORIENTAL

① | 1 1/2 CUPS CUT CELERY
   | 1 1/2 CUPS CUT GREEN PEPPER

CUT CELERY AND PEPPER INTO 1 INCH SQUARES

② | 3/4 CUPS GREEN ONIONS

USE GREEN END OF ONIONS. SNIP WITH SCISSORS INTO SMALL PIECES.

③ | 1 1/2 CUPS MUSHROOMS

SLICE THIN.

④ | 3 TABLESPOONS BUTTER

MELT IN A SKILLET.

⑤ ADD VEGETABLES. STIR FRY UNTIL THEY ARE WARM AND COATED WITH BUTTER.... ABOUT 2 MINUTES.

⑥ | 3 CUPS COOKED BROWN RICE (PAGE 15)
   | 1/3 CUP TAMARI SAUCE

STIR INTO THE VEGETABLES UNTIL THE RICE IS HOT.

SERVES: 4

MISH MASH

1. 3 ZUCCHINI SQUASH — SLICE $\frac{1}{4}$ INCH THICK.

2. 3 TOMATOES — CUT IN QUARTERS.

3. 2 STALKS CELERY — SLICE THIN.

4. $\frac{1}{2}$ CUP SLICED MUSHROOMS
   $\frac{1}{4}$ TEASPOON OF SEA SALT
   PINCH OF BLACK PEPPER

5. 2 TABLESPOONS SAFFLOWER OIL — HEAT IN SKILLET.

6. PUT ABOVE INGREDIENTS INTO HOT SKILLET. STIR AND FRY FOR ABOUT 2 MINUTES. VEGETABLES SHOULD BE VERY HOT BUT STILL CRISP.

7. 1 CUP GRATED CHEESE — STIR INTO HOT VEGETABLES.

SERVES: 4

POCKET BREAD

1. WARM A LARGE BOWL BY FILLING IT WITH HOT WATER. LET SIT FOR 1 MINUTE.

2.
   - 2 TABLESPOONS HONEY
   - 1 CUP HOT WATER
   - 2 PACKAGES DRY YEAST

   MIX INGREDIENTS IN THE BOWL UNTIL THE YEAST AND HONEY ARE DISSOLVED.

3. LET SIT IN A WARM PLACE FOR 5 MINUTES.

4.
   - 1 EGG
   - 3 CUPS WHOLE WHEAT FLOUR
   - 2 TEASPOONS SEA SALT

   ADD TO THE BOWL. STIR IN UNTIL INGREDIENTS ARE WELL MIXED.

5.
   - $\frac{1}{4}$ CUP WHOLE WHEAT FLOUR

   SPRINKLE ONTO BREAD BOARD.

6. PUT DOUGH ON FLOURED BREADBOARD. KNEAD 20 TIMES. TURN DOUGH OVER EACH TIME YOU KNEAD. MOST OF THE FLOUR FROM THE BOARD WILL BE WORKED INTO THE DOUGH.

7. ROLL THE DOUGH INTO SEPARATE LITTLE BALLS—ABOUT THE SIZE OF GOLF BALLS.

8. OIL TWO COOKIE SHEETS.

9. ROLL EACH BALL INTO A CIRCLE $\frac{1}{4}$ INCH THICK WITH A ROLLING PIN. PUT ON COOKIE SHEETS.

POCKET BREAD

⑩ COVER COOKIE SHEETS WITH A CLOTH. PUT IN A WARM (85°) PLACE FOR 1 HOUR.

⑪ TURN ON OVEN TO 500° 10 MINUTES BEFORE YOUR POCKET BREAD IS READY.

⑫ BAKE IN OVEN FOR 10 MINUTES AT 500°.

⑬ WHEN COOL, CUT POCKET BREAD IN HALF. GENTLY INSERT A KNIFE TO OPEN THE INSIDE POCKET.

⑭ STUFF WITH YOUR FAVORITE SANDWICH FILLING.

MAKES: 12

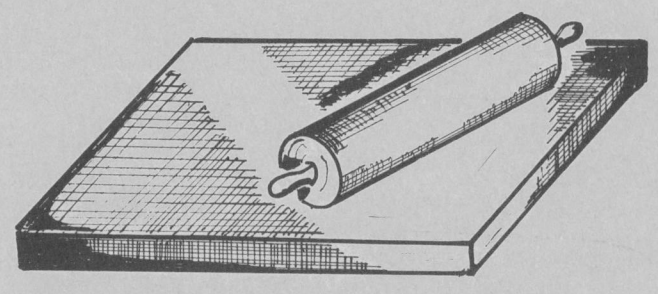

POCKET BREAD FILLINGS

① | 1 AVOCADO | MASH IN A BOWL.

② | 1 TEASPOON LEMON JUICE
PINCH OF SEA SALT
PINCH OF PEPPER | ADD. MIX WELL.

③ | $\frac{1}{2}$ CUP DICED TOMATOES | STIR INTO MIX.

④ | $\frac{1}{4}$ CUP ALFALFA SPROUTS | TOP EACH POCKET SANDWICH WITH SPROUTS.

OR

$\frac{1}{2}$ CUP PEANUT BUTTER
1 SLICED BANANA
1 TABLESPOON HONEY | STIR TOGETHER.

OR

$\frac{1}{4}$ CUP SUNFLOWER SEEDS
$\frac{1}{2}$ CUP DICED TOMATOES
$\frac{1}{2}$ CUP COTTAGE CHEESE
1 TABLESPOON CHOPPED GREEN ONION
PINCH OF SEA SALT | MIX TOGETHER.

FILL EACH HALF OF YOUR POCKET BREAD WITH 2 TABLESPOONS OF MIX. YOU MAY USE YOUR OWN POCKET BREAD OR PITA BREAD THAT YOU BUY AT THE STORE.

QUESADILLA

(1) | 8 CORN TORTILLAS
    | 1 POUND CHEDDAR
    | CHEESE

CUT CHEESE INTO THIN SLICES. ARRANGE TO COVER TORTILLAS.

(2) PUT UNDER BROILER IN OVEN UNTIL CHEESE IS MELTED.

(3) TAKE OUT OF BROILER WITH A SPATULA.

(4) | 2 CUPS DICED TOMATOES

TOP EACH TORTILLA WITH $\frac{1}{4}$ CUP OF THE DICED TOMATOES.

(5) FOLD IN HALF AND SERVE.

SERVES: 4

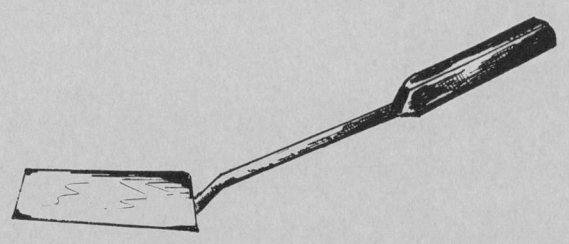

OMELET

① | 1 TEASPOON SAFFLOWER OIL | PUT IN AN 8 INCH SKILLET.

② SWIRL OIL AROUND UNTIL IT COATS THE SIDE AND BOTTOM OF THE SKILLET.

③ PLACE SKILLET ON BURNER. TURN ON HEAT TO HIGH.

④ | 2 EGGS / 1 TEASPOON WATER / PINCH OF SEA SALT | BEAT TOGETHER. POUR INTO HOT SKILLET.

⑤ TURN HEAT DOWN TO LOW. PUT LID ON SKILLET.

⑥ COOK FOR 3 MINUTES. WHEN YOU TAKE THE LID OFF OF THE SKILLET, THE TOP OF THE OMELET SHOULD BE DONE.... NO WET SPOTS.

⑦ COVER $\frac{1}{2}$ OF THE OMELET CIRCLE WITH YOUR FILLING.

⑧ GENTLY FOLD THE OTHER HALF OF THE CIRCLE OVER THE FILLING WITH A SPATULA.

⑨ PUT THE LID ON SKILLET. COOK FOR 1 MORE MINUTE.

MAKES: 1 OMELET

OMELET FILLINGS

> 1/4 CUP APPLESAUCE
> PINCH OF CINNAMON

OR

> 1 OUNCE MONTEREY JACK CHEESE
> 1/4 CUP ALFALFA SPROUTS

OR

> 1 OUNCE CHEEDAR CHEESE
> 1/4 CUP DICED TOMATOES
> PINCH OF SEA SALT

MAKES: FILLING FOR 1 OMELET

USE THESE FILLINGS FOR YOUR OMELETS —— OR —— MAKE UP YOUR OWN. ITS FUN!

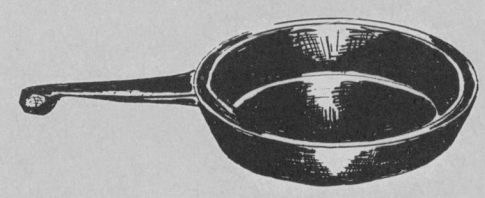

PIZZA SAUCE

① **2 ½ CUPS DICED TOMATOES** — PUT IN A SKILLET. MASH WITH A POTATO MASHER.

② **¼ CUP OLIVE OIL**
1 TEASPOON LEAF OREGANO
1 TEASPOON LEAF BASIL
1 TEASPOON SEA SALT
— STIR INTO THE TOMATOES.

③ TURN HEAT ON HIGH. BRING TO A BOIL. TURN HEAT DOWN. SIMMER FOR 10 MINUTES, STIRRING OCCASIONALLY.

MAKES: 1 ½ CUPS

THIS MAY BE MADE AHEAD AND STORED IN THE REFRIGERATOR.

SUNSHINE PIZZA

① | 6 WHOLE WHEAT ENGLISH MUFFINS | CUT IN HALF.

② | 1 1/2 CUPS PIZZA SAUCE | SPREAD 2 TABLESPOONS OF SAUCE ON EACH MUFFIN HALF.

③ | 3/4 POUND MONTEREY CHEESE | SLICE THIN. PUT A THIN SLICE ON TOP OF EACH MUFFIN HALF.

④ PUT MUFFIN HALVES UNDER BROILER IN OVEN. BROIL UNTIL CHEESE IS MELTED AND EDGES OF YOUR PIZZA ARE TOASTED BROWN.

⑤ | 12 SLICES FRESH TOMATO | PUT 1 SLICE ON EACH COOKED PIZZA.

MAKES: 12 INDIVIDUAL PIZZAS

RAINBOW MACARONI

① TURN ON OVEN TO 350°.

② OIL A 2½ QUART CASSEROLE DISH.

③
| 1½ CUPS VEGETABLE MACARONI
| 2 CUPS GRATED CHEDDAR CHEESE
| ½ TEASPOON SEA SALT
| ¼ TEASPOON PEPPER

STIR TOGETHER IN THE CASSEROLE DISH.

④ 3 CUPS MILK

POUR OVER OTHER INGREDIENTS.

⑤ BAKE 1 HOUR AT 350°.

⑥ TAKE OUT OF THE OVEN. LET SIT FOR 5 MINUTES BEFORE SERVING.

SERVES: 4

DESSERTS

MERINGUE FLUFF

① TURN ON OVEN TO 400°.

② | 3 EGG WHITES | BEAT UNTIL STIFF.

③ | 1 TEASPOON VANILLA
    2 TABLESPOONS HONEY | CONTINUE BEATING EGG WHITES. DRIBBLE IN HONEY. ADD VANILLA. BEAT UNTIL WELL BLENDED.

④ POUR INTO A 5" X 9" LOAF PAN.

⑤ BAKE FOR 10 MINUTES AT 400°.

⑥ COOL FOR 15 MINUTES.

THIS IS SO GOOD SPOONED OVER RICE PUDDING, APPLESAUCE, OR FRESH FRUIT. USE YOUR IMAGINATION!

RICE PUDDING

1. TURN ON OVEN TO 350°.

2. | 3 EGGS | — BEAT IN A LARGE BOWL.

3. | 2 CUPS MILK
   $\frac{3}{4}$ CUP HONEY
   $\frac{1}{4}$ TEASPOON SEA SALT
   $\frac{1}{2}$ TEASPOON NUTMEG
   2 TEASPOONS VANILLA | — STIR INTO EGGS UNTIL WELL BLENDED. YOU MAY USE AN ELECTRIC BEATER SET ON LOW.

4. | 2 CUPS COOKED BROWN RICE (PG. 15) | — STIR IN.

5. POUR INTO AN OILED 9" X 9" PAN.

6. BAKE FOR 1 HOUR AT 350°.

7. TEST PUDDING:
   INSERT KNIFE INTO PUDDING.
   IF KNIFE COMES OUT CLEAN, PUDDING IS DONE.

   IF KNIFE SEEMS TO HAVE PUDDING ON IT, PUT PUDDING BACK INTO OVEN FOR 5 MINUTES. TEST AGAIN.

SERVES: 4

GRANDMA'S APPLESAUCE

① | 5 LARGE APPLES | CAREFULLY CUT IN HALF. CUT OUT CORE. SLICE THIN.

②
- 1/4 TEASPOON SEA SALT
- 1/4 TEASPOON CINNAMON
- 1/2 CUP WATER
- 1/2 CUP HONEY

COMBINE WITH APPLES IN A SAUCEPAN.

③ BRING TO A BOIL. COOK FOR 5 MINUTES, STIRRING OCCASIONALLY.

④ TURN HEAT OFF. PUT LID ON PAN. LET SIT FOR 5 MINUTES.

SERVES: 4

THIS MAY BE SERVED WARM WITH A TABLESPOON OF CREAM IN EACH BOWL; OR CHILL AND SERVE COLD.

IF YOU PREFER A SMOOTH APPLESAUCE, PUT COOKED INGREDIENTS IN A BLENDER. BLEND ON MEDIUM SPEED UNTIL SMOOTH.

STRAWBERRY FLUFF

① | 2 PACKAGES UNFLAVORED GELATIN
    3/4 CUP BOILING WATER | STIR TOGETHER IN A BOWL UNTIL GELATIN IS COMPLETELY DISSOLVED.

② | 1 CUP MASHED STRAWBERRIES
    2/3 CUP HONEY
    1/4 TEASPOON SEA SALT | STIR IN.

③ CHILL IN REFRIGERATOR FOR 30 MINUTES. GELATIN SHOULD BE FIRM.

④ REMOVE FROM REFRIGERATOR. BEAT FOR 3 MINUTES.

⑤ | 1/2 CUP PLAIN YOGURT | STIR IN

⑥ SPOON INTO 4 SMALL BOWLS.

⑦ PUT IN REFRIGERATOR UNTIL READY TO SERVE.

SERVES: 4

CRUNCHY GRANOLA BARS

① TURN ON OVEN TO 350°.

② OIL A 8"X 8" BAKING PAN.

③ | 1 EGG | BEAT EGG IN A LARGE BOWL.

④ | 2 CUPS GRANOLA (PG. 38)
    $\frac{1}{3}$ CUP HONEY
    PINCH OF SEA SALT | ADD TO EGG. MIX WELL.

⑤ PRESS MIXTURE FIRMLY AND EVENLY INTO BAKING PAN.

⑥ BAKE FOR 20 MINUTES AT 350°.

⑦ REMOVE FROM OVEN. LET SIT FOR 15 MINUTES.

⑧ CUT INTO BARS. RUN A KNIFE ALONG THE EDGE OF THE PAN TO LOOSEN BARS FROM THE SIDES.

⑨ LET SIT FOR 15 MINUTES MORE.

⑩ GENTLY REMOVE BARS WITH A SPATULA WHILE STILL WARM.

MAKES: 12 LARGE BARS

LEMON CUSTARD ICE CREAM

① | 3 CUPS WATER | PUT IN THE BOTTOM OF A DOUBLE BOILER. TURN ON HEAT.

② | 3 EGGS | SEPARATE. PUT YOLKS IN 1 BOWL, WHITES IN ANOTHER BOWL.

③ | $\frac{1}{3}$ CUP HONEY
$\frac{1}{3}$ CUP LEMON JUICE
PINCH OF SEA SALT | ADD TO THE BOWL WITH 3 EGG YOLKS. BEAT TOGETHER WELL. POUR INTO TOP PAN OF DOUBLE BOILER.

④ COOK FOR 10 MINUTES. STIR OFTEN WITH A WOODEN SPOON.

⑤ TURN HEAT OFF. CAREFULLY PUT TOP OF DOUBLE BOILER INTO REFRIGERATOR TO COOL INGREDIENTS.

⑥ WITH A CLEAN BEATER, BEAT THE 3 EGG WHITES UNTIL THEY ARE STIFF...... THEY WILL FORM PEAKS.

⑦ | 1 CUP WHIPPING CREAM | IN A SEPARATE BOWL BEAT UNTIL STIFF..... PEAKS WILL FORM.

⑧ POUR COOLED INGREDIENTS FROM REFRIGERATOR (STEP ⑤) INTO WHIPPING CREAM. CAREFULLY FOLD IN. FOLD IN EGG WHITES.

LEMON CUSTARD ICE CREAM

⑨ POUR INTO A BREAD PAN OR SMALL CASSEROLE DISH. YOUR ICE CREAM WILL BE STREAKED WITH PRETTY YELLOW.

⑩ PUT IN FREEZER FOR 3 OR MORE HOURS.

SERVES: 4

CAROB SWIRL ICE CREAM

① USE THE RECIPE FOR LEMON CUSTARD ICE CREAM EXCEPT:

② SUBSTITUTE THE FOLLOWING STEP ③ IN PLACE OF THE LEMON CUSTARD STEP ③.

③
- $\frac{1}{3}$ CUP HONEY
- $\frac{1}{3}$ CUP MILK
- 2 TABLESPOONS CAROB POWDER
- PINCH OF SEA SALT

ADD TO THE BOWL WITH 3 EGG YOLKS. BEAT TOGETHER WELL. POUR INTO TOP PAN OF DOUBLE BOILER.

④ COMPLETE THE STEPS IN THE LEMON CUSTARD ICE CREAM RECIPE.

ANGEL PUFFS

① TURN OVEN ON TO 350.

② | 2 EGG WHITES
   | DASH SEA SALT

BEAT WITH AN ELECTRIC BEATER UNTIL STIFF.

③ | 2 TABLESPOONS HONEY
   | $\frac{1}{2}$ TABLESPOON CAROB POWDER

CONTINUE BEATING WHILE SLOWLY ADDING INGREDIENT.

④ | $\frac{1}{2}$ CUP CHOPPED WALNUTS

FOLD IN.

⑤ COVER COOKIE SHEET WITH WAXED PAPER. PLACE TEASPOONS OF BATTER ABOUT 1 INCH APART ON COOKIE SHEET.

⑥ PLACE IN OVEN. TURN DOWN HEAT TO 200. BAKE FOR $1\frac{1}{2}$ HOURS.

⑦ TAKE OUT OF OVEN. LET COOL FOR 2 MINUTES.

⑧ WITH A METAL SPATULA REMOVE ANGEL PUFFS FROM COOKIE SHEET.

⑨ STORE IN AN AIRTIGHT CONTAINER.

MAKES: 2 DOZEN

SNACKS

TRAIL MIX

(1)
- 1 CUP RAISINS
- $\frac{1}{2}$ CUP ROASTED PEANUTS
- $\frac{1}{2}$ CUP RAW SUNFLOWER SEEDS
- $\frac{1}{2}$ CUP CHOPPED WALNUTS

MIX TOGETHER.

MAKES: $2\frac{1}{2}$ CUPS

POPCORN

(1)
| 1/4 CUP POPCORN |
| 1 TABLESPOON SAFFLOWER OIL |

PUT IN A LIGHTWEIGHT PAN. PLACE LID ON PAN. PUT PAN ON STOVE OVER MEDIUM HEAT.

(2) WHEN YOU HEAR THE FIRST KERNAL "POP" REMOVE FROM HEAT. COUNT TO 60.

(3) RETURN TO BURNER. SHAKE UNTIL THE POPPING STOPS.

(4) POUR INTO A LARGE BOWL. SALT TO YOUR LIKING.

MAKES: 5 CUPS

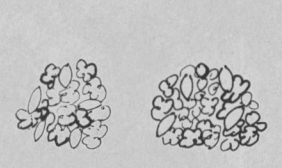

POPCORN BALLS

1. HOT HONEY CAN BURN YOU VERY BADLY. NEVER TOUCH HONEY WHEN IT IS HOT.

2. | 1 CUP HONEY |

   PUT IN A SAUCEPAN. BRING TO A BOIL WHILE STIRRING WITH A WOODEN SPOON.

3. TURN HEAT TO VERY LOW. COOK FOR 5 MINUTES WHILE STIRRING.

4. REMOVE FROM HEAT. LET SIT FOR 2 MINUTES TO COOL.

5. | 5 CUPS POPPED CORN |
   | $\frac{1}{2}$ CUP PEANUTS |
   | $\frac{1}{4}$ TEASPOON SEA SALT |

   PLACE IN A BOWL.

6. DRIBBLE COOKED HONEY OVER POPCORN AND PEANUTS. STIR UNTIL EVERTHING IS COATED WITH HONEY.

7. LET SIT FOR 10 MINUTES TO COOL.

8. BUTTER YOUR HANDS. FORM THE MIXTURE INTO BALLS.

MAKES: 12 POPCORN BALLS

GRANOLA

① TURN ON OVEN TO 250°.

②
| 2 CUPS ROLLED OATS |
| 1/4 CUP SESAME SEEDS |
| 1/2 CUP CHOPPED RAW PEANUTS |
| 1/2 CUP RAW SUNFLOWER SEEDS |
| 1/4 TEASPOON SEA SALT |
| 2 TEASPOONS VANILLA |
| 2 TEASPOONS CINNAMON |
| 1/2 CUP HONEY |
| 1/4 CUP SAFFLOWER OIL |

COMBINE ALL INGREDIENTS IN A LARGE BOWL. WORK INGREDIENTS TOGETHER WITH YOUR HANDS UNTIL IT IS WELL MIXED.

③ SPREAD OUT ON A COOKIE SHEET.

④ BAKE 2 HOURS AT 250°.

⑤ STIR THE MIXTURE EVERY 1/2 HOUR SO IT WILL BROWN EVENLY.

⑥ AS SOON AS YOU TAKE YOUR GRANOLA OUT OF THE OVEN USE A SPATULA TO LOOSEN IT. PUT IT IN A BOWL TO COOL.

MAKES: 5 CUPS

CRUNCHY PEANUT BUTTER

① | 1 CUP ROASTED PEANUTS | PUT LID ON BLENDER. TURN ON HIGH. SLOWLY ADD PEANUTS THROUGH HOLE IN TOP.

② STOP BLENDER TWICE TO SCRAPE SIDES DOWN WITH A RUBBER SPATULA.

③ | 3 TABLESPOONS SAFFLOWER OIL | TURN BLENDER TO LOW. SLOWLY ADD OIL THROUGH HOLE IN TOP.

④ STOP BLENDER TWICE TO SCRAPE SIDES DOWN WITH A RUBBER SPATULA.

⑤ SCRAPE INTO A JAR WITH A RUBBER SPATULA. COVER. STORE IN A REFRIGERATOR.

MAKES: 1 CUP

SNAPPY CHEESE CRACKERS

1. | 1/2 POUND MEDIUM SHARP CHEDDAR CHEESE | — CAREFULLY GRATE CHEESE INTO A LARGE BOWL.

2. | 1/4 CUP BUTTER | — ADD TO BOWL. BUTTER SHOULD BE AT ROOM TEMPERATURE SO IT IS SLIGHTLY SOFT.

3. | 1 TEASPOON WATER
   3/4 CUP WHOLE WHEAT FLOUR
   1/8 TEASPOON CAYENNE PEPPER
   PINCH OF SEA SALT | — MIX ALL INGREDIENTS TOGETHER WITH YOUR HANDS.

4. KEEP WORKING THE MIX UNTIL YOU CAN FORM A BALL THAT STICKS TOGETHER.

5. PUT BALL ON A SMOOTH SURFACE. MAKE A ROLL AS IF YOU WERE MAKING A SNAKE OUT OF CLAY. THE ROLL SHOULD BE ABOUT 15 INCHES LONG.

6. REFRIGERATE THE ROLL FOR 1 HOUR.

7. TURN ON OVEN TO 400°.

8. SLICE ROLL INTO THIN 1/4 INCH SLICES. PLACE ON OILED COOKIE SHEET.

SNAPPY CHEESE CRACKERS

⑨ BAKE CRACKERS FOR 12 MINUTES AT 400°.

⑩ STORE IN AN AIRTIGHT CONTAINER.

MAKES: 4 DOZEN

IF AFTER A FEW DAYS YOUR CRACKERS LOSE THEIR CRISPNESS JUST POP THEM BACK IN THE OVEN ON A COOKIE SHEET. BAKE FOR 5 MINUTES AT 350°.

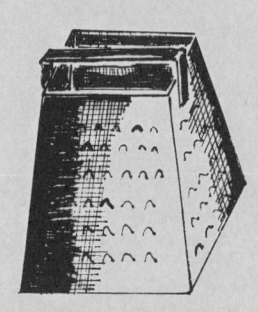

CINNAMON NUT BUNS

① | 4 WHOLE WHEAT ENGLISH MUFFINS / BUTTER | CUT IN HALF. BUTTER EACH MUFFIN HALF EVENLY.

② | 1 CUP CHOPPED WALNUTS

③ SPREAD WALNUTS EVENLY ON A CLEAN FLAT SURFACE. PRESS BUTTERED SIDE OF EACH ENGLISH MUFFIN FIRMLY INTO THE CHOPPED WALNUTS.

④ | $\frac{1}{4}$ CUP HONEY / 2 TEASPOONS CINNAMON / $\frac{1}{4}$ TEASPOON NUTMEG | MIX WELL.

⑤ DRIZZLE $\frac{1}{2}$ TABLESPOON OF THE MIXTURE OVER THE WALNUTS ON EACH MUFFIN HALF.

⑥ BROIL UNTIL SLIGHTLY TOASTED.

MAKES: 8 BUNS

PARTY SURPRISE

① | 1 LOAF UNSLICED WHOLE WHEAT OR RYE BREAD | TRIM OFF CRUST. CUT BREAD INTO 1 INCH SQUARES.

② | 3 CUPS WATER | PUT IN BOTTOM OF DOUBLE BOILER. TURN ON HEAT.

③ | $\frac{3}{4}$ CUP BUTTER
12 OUNCES CHEDDAR CHEESE
PINCH OF CAYENNE PEPPER
PINCH OF SEA SALT | CRUMBLE CHEESE INTO TOP OF DOUBLE BOILER. ADD OTHER INGREDIENTS.

④ STIR OCCASIONALLY UNTIL INGREDIENTS ARE MELTED TOGETHER.

⑤ | 2 EGG WHITES | BEAT UNTIL STIFF. FOLD INTO CHEESE MIXTURE.

⑥ DIP EACH SQUARE OF BREAD INTO THE CHEESE MIXTURE WITH A FORK. PUT ON A COOKIE SHEET.

⑦ PLACE IN REFRIGERATOR FOR 4 HOURS.

⑧ BAKE FOR 12 MINUTES AT 350°.

MAKES: 3 DOZEN

FRUIT LEATHER

(1) | 4 RIPE PEARS | CUT OUT CORE. CUT INTO SLICES.

(2) | 1 TABLESPOON HONEY / 1 TABLESPOON WATER | PUT IN BLENDER. PUT LID ON.

(3) ADD THE FRUIT THROUGH THE HOLE IN THE BLENDER LID.

(4) STOP THE BLENDER. SCRAPE THE SIDES WITH A RUBBER SPATULA. TURN BLENDER ON. ADD MORE FRUIT.

(5) REPEAT STEP (4) UNTIL YOU HAVE 2 CUPS OF PULP.

(6) OIL A COOKIE SHEET.

(7) SPREAD PULP OUT ON THE COOKIE SHEET. IT SHOULD BE NO THICKER THAN $\frac{1}{4}$ INCH.

(8) TURN THE OVEN ON TO LOW. PUT COOKIE SHEET IN THE OVEN. LEAVE THE OVEN DOOR SLIGHTLY OPEN.

(9) LEAVE IN OVEN FOR 8 HOURS TO DRY.

(10) GENTLY PEEL LEATHER FROM COOKIE SHEET. ROLL LEATHER INTO A TUBE. STORE IN AN AIRTIGHT CONTAINER.

YOU MAY USE OTHER FRUITS, SUCH AS APRICOTS, PEACHES, OR APPLESAUCE, FOR YOUR FRUIT LEATHER.

MAGIC MIX

MAGIC MIX

Has your family ever bought Bisquick or pancake mix to save time?

Now you can make your own MAGIC MIX to help you save time. And your MAGIC MIX is made with whole wheat flour, has no preservatives, and is good for you.

With your MAGIC MIX you can make pancakes, muffins, cornbread, cookies and on and on.

MAGIC MIX

①
- 6 CUPS WHOLE WHEAT FLOUR
- 1 CUP NON-INSTANT DRY MILK
- 2 TEASPOONS SEA SALT
- 2 TABLESPOONS BAKING POWDER

PUT IN A LARGE BOWL.

② 1 CUP SAFFLOWER OIL

<u>SLOWLY DRIZZLE</u> OVER ABOVE INGREDIENTS WHILE USING A PASTRY BLENDER TO WORK ALL INGREDIENTS TOGETHER WELL.

③ STORE IN AN AIRTIGHT CONTAINER IN YOUR REFRIGERATOR.

MAKES: 6 CUPS

ABRACADABRA...... YOU HAVE YOUR OWN MAGIC MIX

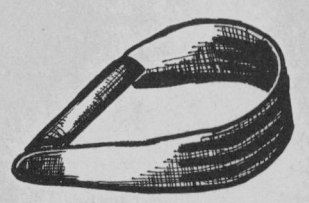

MAGIC MIX BANANA NUT BREAD

① TURN ON OVEN TO 350°.

②
```
2 EGGS
3 BANANAS
3/4 CUP HONEY
1 TEASPOON VANILLA
2 TEASPOONS CINNAMON
```
BEAT TOGETHER IN A BIG BOWL UNTIL BANANAS ARE IN SMALL LUMPS.

③
```
2 CUPS MAGIC MIX
```
ADD. BEAT LIGHTLY UNTIL WELL MIXED.

④
```
1/2 CUP RAISINS
```
STIR IN.

⑤ OIL A 5" X 9" LOAF PAN. POUR IN BATTER.

⑥ BAKE FOR 1 HOUR AT 350°.

⑦ TEST.
   INSERT A TOOTHPICK INTO THE BREAD:
      IF IT COMES OUT CLEAN YOUR BREAD IS DONE.

      IF IT SEEMS TO HAVE BATTER ON IT, PUT BREAD BACK INTO THE OVEN FOR 5 MORE MINUTES. TEST AGAIN.

⑧ LET SIT FOR 10 MINUTES BEFORE TAKING BREAD OUT OF PAN. GENTLY LOOSEN WITH RUBBER SPATULA.

MAKES: 1 LOAF

MAGIC MIX PANCAKES

①
- 2 EGGS
- $\frac{3}{4}$ CUP WATER
- 2 TABLESPOONS HONEY

BEAT TOGETHER IN A LARGE BOWL.

② $1\frac{1}{2}$ CUPS MAGIC MIX

ADD TO INGREDIENTS IN BOWL. BEAT SLOWLY UNTIL WELL BLENDED.

③ OIL YOUR GRIDDLE. WIPE WELL WITH A PAPER TOWEL THAT HAS BEEN DIPPED IN SAFFLOWER OIL.

④ TEST YOUR GRIDDLE.
TURN HEAT ON HIGH. SPLASH A DROP OF WATER ON YOUR GRIDDLE. THE WATER WILL DANCE... DANCE... DANCE WHEN YOUR GRIDDLE IS READY. <u>THEN</u> TURN THE HEAT DOWN.

⑤ USE $\frac{1}{4}$ CUP MEASURING CUP TO POUR YOUR BATTER ON THE GRIDDLE.

⑥ WHEN THE TOP OF THE PANCAKE BUBBLES GENTLY TURN IT OVER WITH A SPATULA TO BROWN THE OTHER SIDE.

⑦ REOIL YOUR GRIDDLE OFTEN.

MAKES: 8-10 PANCAKES

SERVE WITH HONEY BUTTER OR APPLESAUCE HONEY SYRUP.

APPLESAUCE HONEY SYRUP

① | 1/2 CUP APPLESAUCE
  | 1/2 CUP HONEY

HEAT TOGETHER IN A SAUCEPAN.

② SERVE HOT.

MAKES: 1 CUP

HONEY BUTTER

① | 1/2 CUP HONEY
  | 1 CUBE BUTTER

MELT TOGETHER IN A SAUCEPAN.

② SERVE HOT.

MAKES: 1 CUP

MAGIC MIX PEANUT BUTTER COOKIES

① | 1 EGG | BEAT IN A LARGE BOWL.

② | 1 CUP PEANUT BUTTER
    $\frac{3}{4}$ CUP HONEY | BEAT TOGETHER WITH EGG.

③ | $2\frac{1}{2}$ CUPS MAGIC MIX | ADD. STIR UNTIL WELL BLENDED.

④ COVER BOWL. PUT IN REFRIGERATOR FOR 1 HOUR.

⑤ TURN ON OVEN TO 350°.

⑥ OIL A COOKIE SHEET.

⑦ FORM DOUGH INTO WALNUT SIZED BALLS. PLACE ON COOKIE SHEET ABOUT 2 INCHES APART.

⑧ DIP A FORK IN FLOUR. PRESS EACH BALL FLAT.

⑨ BAKE FOR 10 MINUTES AT 350°.

⑩ REFRIGERATE DOUGH BETWEEN BATCHES.

MAKES: 3 DOZEN

MAGIC MIX APPLE MUFFINS

① TURN ON OVEN TO 375°.

② OIL YOUR MUFFIN TIN. WIPE LIGHTLY WITH A PAPER TOWEL THAT HAS BEEN DIPPED IN SAFFLOWER OIL.

③ NOW PUT A PINCH OF FLOUR IN EACH CUP. SHAKE MUFFIN TIN UNTIL SIDES AND BOTTOM ARE COATED WITH FLOUR.

④
- 2 CUPS MAGIC MIX
- 2 EGGS
- $\frac{1}{2}$ CUP APPLE JUICE
- $\frac{1}{4}$ CUP HONEY
- 1 TEASPOON VANILLA
- $\frac{1}{2}$ TEASPOON CINNAMON

BEAT TOGETHER IN A LARGE BOWL.

⑤ 1 APPLE

TAKE OUT CORE. CUT INTO SMALL PIECES. STIR INTO ABOVE MIX.

⑥ $\frac{1}{4}$ CUP CHOPPED WALNUTS.   STIR IN.

⑦ FILL MUFFIN CUPS $\frac{2}{3}$ FULL.

⑧ BAKE FOR 25 MINUTES AT 375°.

MAKES: 12

MAGIC MIX CREPES

① | 1 EGG
    1 TABLESPOON HONEY
    1/2 CUP PUREED
        APPLESAUCE   BEAT TOGETHER IN A LARGE BOWL.

② | 3/4 CUP MAGIC MIX   ADD. BEAT WELL.

③ LIGHTLY OIL AN 8 INCH SKILLET.

④ HEAT UNTIL A DROP OF WATER WILL DANCE ON THE SKILLET.

⑤ POUR 1/4 CUP OF BATTER INTO THE SKILLET. GENTLY ROLL THE SKILLET UNTIL THE BATTER IS SPREAD EVENLY.

⑥ COOK UNTIL THE TOP OF THE CREPE BUBBLES AND BECOMES DULL. GENTLY PEEL CREPE FROM THE SKILLET.

⑦ STACK CREPES TOGETHER WITH WAX PAPER BETWEEN EACH CREPE.

⑧ FILL CREPE WITH YOUR FAVORITE FILLING.

MAKES: 8 CREPES

CREPE FILLINGS

① | 1 CUP APPLESAUCE | FILL EACH CREPE WITH 2 TABLESPOONS OF APPLESAUCE.

② | $\frac{1}{2}$ CUP GRANOLA (PG. 38) | SPRINKLE 1 TABLESPOON OF GRANOLA OVER APPLESAUCE.

③ GENTLY FOLD CREPE OVER.

OR

① | 1 RECIPE MERINGUE FLUFF (PG. 27) | SPOON AS MUCH AS YOU LIKE INTO EACH CREPE.

② GENTLY FOLD CREPE OVER.

AND

① | 1 TABLESPOON LEMON JUICE
$\frac{1}{2}$ CUP HONEY | BLEND TOGETHER.

② DRIZZLE 1 TABLESPOON OF LEMON HONEY OVER EACH FILLED CREPE JUST BEFORE SERVING.

                        FILLS: 8 CREPES

MAGIC MIX CORNBREAD

① TURN ON OVEN TO 400°.

② PUT 1 TEASPOON SAFFLOWER OIL IN A 9" X 9" PAN. WIPE AROUND WITH A PAPER TOWEL TO OIL THE PAN.

③ | 2 EGGS
    3 TABLESPOONS HONEY | BEAT TOGETHER IN A BOWL.

④ | 1 CUP WATER
    1 $\frac{1}{2}$ CUPS MAGIC MIX
    1 CUP CORNMEAL | ADD AND BEAT ON LOW UNTIL WELL BLENDED.

⑤ POUR INTO PAN.

⑥ BAKE FOR 25 MINUTES AT 400°.

⑦ TEST.
   INSERT A TOOTHPICK INTO THE BREAD:
      IF IT COMES OUT CLEAN, YOUR BREAD IS DONE.

      IF IT SEEMS TO HAVE BATTER ON IT, PUT CORNBREAD BACK INTO THE OVEN FOR 5 MORE MINUTES. THEN TEST AGAIN.

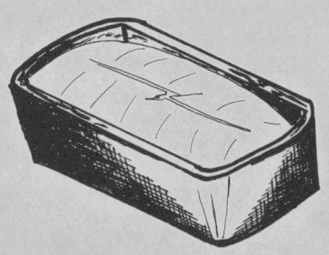

SERVES: 6

BE AN ACCURATE COOK

TO MEASURE LIQUIDS

FILL MEASURING SPOONS TO THE TOP. USE A MEASURING CUP THAT'S MEANT FOR LIQUIDS (TRANSPARENT). PUT THE CUP ON A LEVEL SURFACE. LOOK THROUGH THE CUP WITH YOUR EYE AT THE SAME LEVEL AS THE LIQUID TO MAKE SURE YOU HAVE THE CORRECT MEASUREMENT.

TO MEASURE DRY INGREDIENTS

GENTLY FILL MEASURING SPOON OR MEASURING CUP WITH THE INGREDIENT. DON'T PACK IT DOWN. LEVEL OFF WITH A SPATULA OR TABLE KNIFE.

TO MEASURE BUTTER

PACK BUTTER INTO EITHER THE MEASURING SPOON OR CUP. LEVEL OFF WITH SPATULA OR TABLE KNIFE. OR USE THE TABLE BELOW.

MEASUREMENTS

3 TEASPOONS	=	1 TABLESPOON
4 TABLESPOONS	=	$\frac{1}{4}$ CUP
16 TABLESPOONS	=	1 CUP
4 CUPS	=	1 QUART
$\frac{1}{2}$ CUP BUTTER	=	1 CUBE OF BUTTER

SOME COOKING TERMS

BEAT....... USE HAND BEATERS OR AN ELECTRIC BEATER.

BEAT UNTIL STIFF...... STIFF LITTLE PEAKS WILL FORM.

BOIL....... HEAT UNTIL IT BUBBLES.

CHOP...... CUT INTO SMALL PIECES.

COMBINE... PUTTING SEVERAL FOODS TOGETHER.

DICE...... CUT INTO SMALL CUBES.

FOLD...... PUTTING FOODS TOGETHER BY GENTLY FOLDING ONE PART OVER THE OTHER WITH A SPOON.

GRATE...... USING A GRATER. A PLASTIC ONE IS SAFER. YOU CAN ALSO USE SOME BLENDERS TO GRATE FOODS.

KNEAD..... WORKING AND STRETCHING DOUGH. FOLD THE DOUGH IN HALF. PRESS IT WITH THE PALMS OF YOUR HANDS. TURN THE DOUGH AROUND SLIGHTLY. REPEAT.

MIX........ STIR WITH A SPOON.

OIL........ PUT A TEASPOON OF SAFFLOWER OIL IN YOUR PAN. WIPE THE OIL AROUND UNTIL THE PAN IS COATED EVENLY.
FOR BREADS:
SHAKE FLOUR ONTO AN OILED PAN. SHAKE PAN UNTIL THE FLOUR COATS THE PAN EVENLY.

PINCH.......	AS MUCH AS YOU CAN PINCH BETWEEN YOUR THUMB AND FINGER.
PUREE.......	TO MAKE SMOOTH IN A BLENDER OR A FOOD PRESS.
SEPARATE EGGS	YOU NEED TWO BOWLS. CRACK AN EGG AGAINST THE SIDE OF ONE BOWL. WITH YOUR FINGERS HELD LOOSELY TOGETHER, OPEN THE EGG SHELL. LET THE WHITE SLIDE THROUGH YOUR FINGERS INTO THE BOWL. GENTLY HOLD THE YOLK. DON'T BREAK THE YOLK. (YOLK IN EGG WHITES PREVENTS THE WHITES FROM BEATING UNTIL STIFF). PUT THE YOLK INTO THE OTHER BOWL.
TIME........	WATCH THE CLOCK. A TIMER YOU CAN SET TAKES AWAY THE WORRY OF LOOKING AT THE CLOCK. A TIMER IS THE COOK'S GOOD FRIEND.